STATE AND COUNTY COURTS

BARBARA M. LINDE

PowerKiDS
press.

NEW YORK

Published in 2020 by The Rosen Publishing Group, Inc.
29 East 21st Street, New York, NY 10010

Editor: Jane Katirgis
Book Design: Rachel Rising

Photo Credits: Cover Tammy Venable/Shutterstock.com; Cover, pp. 1, 3, 4, 5, 6, 7, 8, 9, 10, 11, 12, 13, 14, 15, 16, 17, 18, 19, 20, 21, 22, 23, 24, 25, 26, 27, 28, 29, 30, 31, 32 (background) Allgusak/Shutterstock.com; pp. 5, 23 wavebreakmedia/Shutterstock.com; pp. 6, 10, 12, 14, 20, 24, 26 (gavel) AVA Bitter/Shutterstock.com; p. 7 https://commons.wikimedia.org/wiki/File:Pitt_County_Courthouse.JPG; p. 8 rawf8 /Shutterstock.com; p. 9 Kubko/ Shutterstock.com; p. 11 Macrovector/Shutterstock.com; p. 13 Freeograph/Shutterstock.com; p. 15 Casper1774 Studio/ Shutterstock.com; p. 17 Universal History Archive/Universal Images Group/Getty Images; p. 18 hafakot/Shutterstock. com; p. 19 eurobanks/Shutterstock.com; p. 21 Michael Rosebrock/Shutterstock.com; p. 25 Library of Congress/ Corbis Historical/Getty Images; p. 27 New York Daily News Archive/Contributor/Getty Images; p. 29 https://commons. wikimedia.org/wiki/File:Official_Presidential_portrait_of_John_Adams_(by_John_Trumbull,_circa_1792).jpg; p. 29 https://commons.wikimedia.org/wiki/File:AbrahamLincolnOilPainting1869Restored.jpg; p. 29 https://commons. wikimedia.org/wiki/File:President_Barack_Obama.jpg; p. 29 (background) arigato/Shutterstock.com; p. 30 Lana U/ Shutterstock.com.

Library of Congress Cataloging-in-Publication Data

Names: Linde, Barbara M., author.
Title: State and county courts / Barbara M. Linde.
Description: New York : PowerKids Press, 2020. | Series: Court is in session
   | Includes index.
Identifiers: LCCN 2018036229| ISBN 9781538343302 (library bound) | ISBN
   9781538343289 (pbk.) | ISBN 9781538343296 (6 pack)
Subjects: LCSH: Courts—United States—Juvenile literature. | Justice,
   Administration of—United States—Juvenile literature. | State
   courts—United States--Juvenile literature. | County courts—United
   States—Juvenile literature.
Classification: LCC KF8700 .L56 2019 | DDC 347.73/3—dc23
LC record available at https://lccn.loc.gov/2018036229

Acknowledgments
The author thanks the following attorneys for their input:
Deborah A. Lott, Trust and Probate Administrator, Zaremba Center for Estate Planning and Elder Law, Williamsburg, Virginia; Mark Schmidt, Attorney at Law, Newport News, Virginia.

Manufactured in the United States of America

CPSIA Compliance Information: Batch #CSPK19. For further information contact Rosen Publishing, New York, New York at 1-800-237-9932.

Contents

WHAT IS A STATE COURT SYSTEM?

Fifty states and five territories in the United States have their own court system. Each system was established by the state or territory's constitution. State courts hear cases that aren't covered by federal courts. Many of these matters have to do with the daily lives of people who live in that state.

The state courts are part of the judicial branch of the state's government. This is the branch that decides whether the state's laws are being followed correctly. The courts have the legal authority to listen to and rule on cases having to do with civil or criminal matters. Civil cases have to do with conflicts between two parties. Criminal cases have to do with those accused of breaking laws.

Each state has several different levels of courts. Each level has jurisdiction, or authority, over certain kinds of cases.

THREE BRANCHES

Each state has three branches of government. The executive branch, headed by the governor, carries out the laws. The legislative branch makes the laws. The judicial branch interprets, or explains the meaning of, the laws.

Two attorneys, or lawyers, speak with a judge in a courtroom.

STATES AND COUNTIES

States are divided into smaller geographical areas to make running the state easier. In 48 states, these areas are called "counties." In Louisiana, these divisions are called "parishes." They're called "boroughs" in Alaska. Each county has its own government.

Each state is independent and allowed to make any laws or rules that don't go against the U.S. Constitution or its state constitution. Therefore, state laws can vary greatly from state to state.

What About the Name?

Before Louisiana became part of the United States, France and then Spain owned the territory. Both were Catholic countries that divided the land into parishes, which were areas that had a church and a priest. When Louisiana became a state, it kept the name "parishes" for its divisions. When Alaska became a state, its leaders decided to use the term "borough." They wanted the state's organization to be different from that of the rest of the states, and they wanted the divisions to have different roles and powers than counties.

This photo shows the Pitt County Courthouse in Greenville, Pitt County, North Carolina.

One county responsibility is the **administration** of the lower state courts. These courts have jurisdiction only in the county where they're located. Each county usually has an official building called a courthouse where the court sits, or meets.

The state also administers the highest state court, which is usually called the state supreme court.

AN EXAMPLE COURT SYSTEM

Let's take a look at one state as an example. Virginia is organized into 32 judicial districts. Each city or county is in one of these districts. The Virginia court system has four levels.

First are the general district courts. One operates independently in each district and hears cases involving minor crimes and civil cases. Next, each district has circuit courts that hear **felony** cases and larger civil cases. If the parties in a district court case disagree about a ruling, they appeal the decision to the circuit court. This court hears the case and either upholds the old decision or gives a new one.

DIAGRAM OF THE VIRGINIA COURT SYSTEM

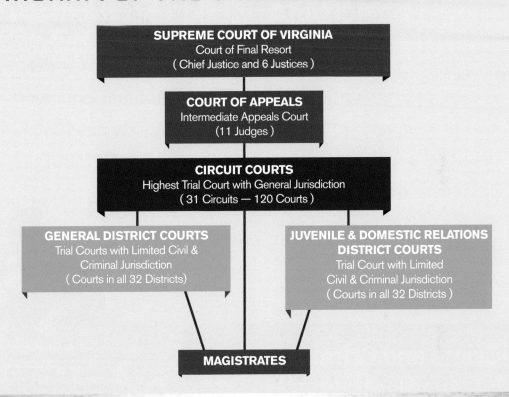

SUPREME COURT OF VIRGINIA
Court of Final Resort
(Chief Justice and 6 Justices)

COURT OF APPEALS
Intermediate Appeals Court
(11 Judges)

CIRCUIT COURTS
Highest Trial Court with General Jurisdiction
(31 Circuits — 120 Courts)

GENERAL DISTRICT COURTS
Trial Courts with Limited Civil &
Criminal Jurisdiction
(Courts in all 32 Districts)

JUVENILE & DOMESTIC RELATIONS DISTRICT COURTS
Trial Court with Limited
Civil & Criminal Jurisdiction
(Courts in all 32 Districts)

MAGISTRATES

There is one court of appeals that reviews appeals of circuit court decisions. Finally, the state supreme court hears appeals from the court of appeals. It also hears cases that have to do with the behavior of lawyers, judges, and other government officials.

GENERAL DISTRICT COURTS

The general district court is the lowest-level court. A case or a lawsuit starts here. The exact matters these courts hear vary from state to state, but they usually hear civil cases that involve less than about $25,000. In criminal cases, these courts handle less serious crimes called misdemeanors.

Crime and Criminals

A crime is a behavior that is harmful to people or society. Each state has laws usually called the criminal code. The laws explain which offenses are criminal and may suggest punishments. The state government is the **prosecutor**. It charges the defendant, who is the person accused of breaking the law. The government might decide not to go to trial. The defendant may make a plea bargain, admitting guilt to a more minor charge to get a smaller punishment.

A courtroom might have a layout that looks like this.

JUDGE

VICTIM

ATTORNEY

JURY

WITNESS

The purpose of a civil trial is to make sure that a disagreement is settled justly, according to the state's laws. The person bringing the case is called the plaintiff, and the other person is the **defendant**. Attorneys for both sides will present evidence and interview witnesses. Depending on the type of case, a judge alone might hear the case and make a ruling called a verdict, or a jury may be involved.

FAMILY AND JUVENILE COURTS

Family and juvenile courts are lower civil trial courts that only have jurisdiction over family or juvenile matters. Family courts cover child **custody** and support payments if family members don't live together. They also cover cases about **abuse** and neglect. The judges are often experts in family law, and they do their best to rule for the good of all family members.

Juvenile courts deal with young people, usually from the ages of 7 to 17. When a juvenile commits a crime, the case is called a juvenile delinquency case. The young person isn't treated the same

Who Is a Juvenile?

The upper age limit to go into juvenile court is 17 in 41 states and the District of Columbia. Only North Carolina and New York set the age at 15. The remaining seven states set the age at 16.

A family speaks with a judge in family court.

way an adult criminal would be treated. Most juvenile offenses have to do with stealing, assault, use of drugs, or truancy, which means not going to school. Usually a judge, not a jury, hears juvenile cases.

PROBATE AND TRAFFIC COURTS

Traffic courts and probate courts are also lower-level trial courts. They have limited jurisdiction, and judges hear the cases. When someone dies, they often leave money, property, and unpaid bills. They may have a will that explains who should get their things and take care of their affairs. People who are named in the will, or those who are left out of it, may disagree with what the will says. A probate court takes care of these matters.

Wills: Handle with Care

It's important to treat a will with special care. For example, in New York, if someone takes staples out of the pages of a will and then re-staples them, they have to give the court a special statement called an **affidavit**. They must explain why they removed the staples, tell where they kept the will, and swear that they know of no changes being made. The affidavit has to be signed in front of a notary public, a person with the state's authority to serve as a witness.

A last will and testament, or will, tells a person's final wishes.

Last Will and Testament

I, an adult residing at Santa Monica, Califonia, being of sound mind, declare this to be my Last Will and Testament. I revoke all wills and codicils previously made by me.

ARTICLE I

I appoint my son as my Personal Representative to administer this Will, and ask that he/s ... permitted to serve without Court supervision and without posting bond. If my so ... ...nable to serve, then I appoint daughter to serve as my Personal Represent ... ...permitted to serve without Court supervision and without ...

... all of the

If a driver gets a ticket for breaking a traffic law, such as a speed limit, the driver can either pay the fine or go to traffic court to ask to have the fine removed. People accused of reckless driving go to traffic court. Drivers who have their driver's license taken away go to court to try to get it back.

CIRCUIT COURTS

Circuit courts usually cover several counties or districts. The number of judges varies by state. They hear civil cases that involve higher amounts of money than those heard in the general district courts. In some states, these courts have jurisdiction over adoptions, divorces, and wills. They handle the more serious criminal cases, called felonies. Juveniles who commit felonies may be tried in a circuit court instead of in juvenile court.

When either or both parties in a general district court case disagree with the judge's verdict, they can appeal the case to the circuit court. The appeal must be filed within a certain amount of time, which varies by state. The circuit court tries the case all over again and issues a verdict.

TRAVELING COURT

The term "circuit court" comes from earlier times when populations were more spread out and there weren't many local courts. Judges and lawyers rode horses or traveled by stagecoach to hear cases in different areas. The route was called a circuit.

This is the Civil Courts Building in St. Louis, Missouri. The 22nd Judicial Circuit Court of Missouri meets here.

COURTS OF APPEALS

The purpose of a court of appeals is to make sure the laws were followed correctly in lower court decisions. Some court of appeals decisions are final, which means the case can't go any higher. Other cases may go on to the state's supreme court. Each state has its own rules about how the cases are handled.

Judges, not juries, hear courts of appeals cases. The number of judges on a court of appeals varies by state. These judges usually work in small groups to review cases. The groups may travel around a state to hear cases, or groups of judges may be located in different areas of a state. Both methods are meant to make it easier for people to use the courts.

FOR ALL TO SEE

In many states, including Michigan and New York, information about the cases and decisions are posted on the court of appeals page of the state courts website. Most of the information is available to the general public.

The District of Columbia Court of Appeals building is where appeals cases are heard in Washington, D.C.

DISTRICT OF COLUMBIA COURT OF APPEALS

LINCOLN

STATE SUPREME COURT

A supreme court is the highest-level court in the state. These courts' main purpose is to review appeals cases from lower courts. They're often called "courts of last resort" because their decisions are final. The only way to appeal a decision by a state's supreme court is to file an appeal with the United States Supreme Court.

Supreme court judges are usually called "justices." The number of justices varies by state. In some states, such as New Mexico, the

The Grocery Bag Case

Paper grocery bags had their day in the Colorado supreme court recently. The Aspen City Council passed an **ordinance** that charged people 20 cents for each paper grocery bag. A group of citizens said the fee was a tax that people had to vote on. The case went through an appeals court to the supreme court. The supreme court ruled in favor of the city council.

Shown here is the Colorado State Supreme Court building in Denver, Colorado.

COLORADO SUPREME COURT
COLORADO COURT OF APPEALS

justices choose one of their members as the chief justice. In others, such as Kansas, the honor goes to the justice who has served the longest. Governors in California and a few other states appoint the chief justice. This person is in charge of the state's judicial system.

SELECTING JUDGES

The selection of judges varies by state, but all states aim to have judges who will apply the laws correctly. In Virginia and South Carolina, the members of the general assembly vote and elect the judges for all the courts. In Massachusetts, the governor appoints all the judges, and the governor's council votes on them. The governor of New Jersey appoints most of the judges there, and the state Senate votes on them. The mayor of each city appoints that city's **municipal** judges.

The people elect their judges in Alabama, Illinois, Pennsylvania, and many other states. In Arizona counties with more than 250,000 people, governors choose judges for certain courts from a list of qualified people. In counties with fewer than 250,000 people, judges run in an election for the positions.

A LIFELONG PROFESSION

In Massachusetts, New Hampshire, and Rhode Island, judges can serve until they are 70 years old. In New Jersey, judges who get a second appointment can serve until age 70. The other states have different lengths for judicial terms.

All judges in all states wear long black robes in court. This tradition started in the early 1800s or before.

A FAMOUS CASE: MURRAY V. PEARSON

In 1935, Donald Gaines Murray was refused entrance to the University of Maryland Law School because he was African American. He sued the state of Maryland and the University of Maryland for **discrimination**. Thurgood Marshall was an African American attorney from Maryland who had earlier been turned down by the university. He and his mentor, Charles Houston, and Nicholas Gosnell, another attorney from Baltimore, took Murray's case. They said the discrimination was

More About Thurgood Marshall

The arguments the attorneys developed helped Marshall when he brought *Brown v. Board of Education* to the U.S. Supreme Court in 1954. The court ruled that **segregation** in public schools was illegal. Marshall went on to serve as the first African American Supreme Court justice from 1967 to 1991.

Left to right: Thurgood Marshall, Donald Gaines Murray, and Charles Houston prepare for court during the *Murray v. Pearson* case.

unconstitutional because the state didn't have a law school for African American students that was equal to the school for the white students.

They won in the first court and in the Maryland Court of Appeals. Raymond Pearson, the president of the university, admitted Murray as a student. The victory also helped **integrate** other University of Maryland schools.

A FAMOUS CASE: TENNESSEE V. JOHN SCOPES

From July 10 to 21, 1925, an important trial took place in a courtroom in Dayton, Tennessee. At the time, Charles Darwin's theory of **evolution** was still rather new, and Tennessee law said teaching it was a misdemeanor. John Scopes was a high school science teacher who taught the theory in spite of the law. He was arrested.

The Monkey Trial

The case was also called "the monkey trial" because Darwin said that people descended from primates, the group that includes apes and monkeys. Many people disagreed because they believed in the biblical story of creation. Because of the guilty verdict, many publishers stopped including evolution in textbooks. The **debate** went on for many years, and by the 1960s, evolution reappeared in textbooks. However, to some extent, the debate still continues.

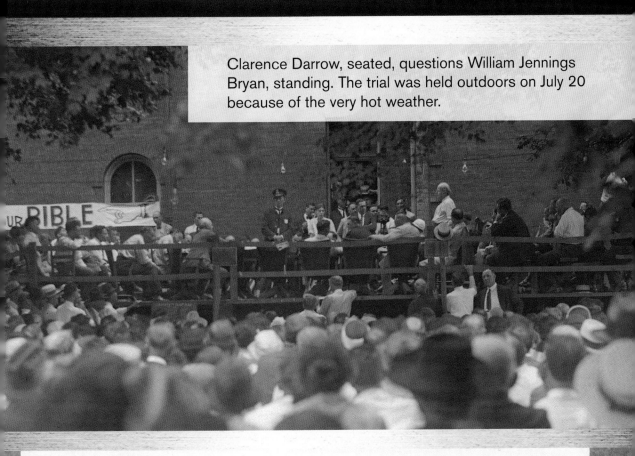

Clarence Darrow, seated, questions William Jennings Bryan, standing. The trial was held outdoors on July 20 because of the very hot weather.

The American Civil Liberties Union, with famous lawyer Clarence Darrow, defended Scopes. The state's prosecutor was another famous lawyer, William Jennings Bryan. While the judge tried to keep the focus on whether Scopes broke the law, both lawyers argued about the theory versus the Bible. The jury found Scopes guilty and fined him $100. He appealed to the Tennessee supreme court, which upheld the law but did away with the verdict because Scopes's fine was too high.

FROM STATE LAWYER TO PRESIDENT

John Adams was the second president of the United States and the first lawyer to hold that office. He practiced law in Massachusetts, starting in 1758. Adams supported the colonies' independence from Great Britain. He wrote the Massachusetts Constitution.

Abraham Lincoln practiced law in Illinois for about 25 years, serving part of that time as a circuit court lawyer. He took all kinds of cases. Lincoln was the 16th president, from 1861 until his assassination in 1865.

Barack Obama practiced law in Illinois from 1993 until 2004, focusing on civil rights cases. He also taught constitutional law at the University of Chicago Law School. Obama became a senator in 2005 and then served as the 44th U.S. president from 2009 to 2017.

LAWYERS IN THE WHITE HOUSE

While a politician doesn't need a background as a lawyer, many politicians are lawyers. Twenty-five of the nation's 45 presidents started as lawyers, including Thomas Jefferson, Woodrow Wilson, Franklin D. Roosevelt, Gerald Ford, and Bill Clinton.

John Adams was president from 1797 to 1801, Abraham Lincoln served from 1861 to 1865, and Barack Obama led the country from 2009 to 2017.

JOHN ADAMS

ABRAHAM LINCOLN

BARACK OBAMA

JUSTICE FOR ALL

Laws are important because they are designed to keep people safe and make sure that everyone's rights are protected. Each state has control over its laws and has an independent court system. The state court system makes sure the state's laws are applied correctly. These courts are busy places, hearing more than 30 million cases every year. The arrangement in levels from the lower courts to the state's supreme court means appeals can be used to review a lower court's decision.

Going to court is probably not high on anyone's list of things to do. However, it helps to know that in every state, there is a court system with a goal of seeing that justice is served. Citizens can have confidence in their state's court system.

GLOSSARY

abuse: The act of treating or using something or someone in a wrong or unfair way.

administration: The activities that relate to running a government, company, school, or other organization.

affidavit: A written statement that's used as evidence in a court of law and is signed by someone who says the information is true.

custody: The legal care and control of a person.

debate: An argument or public discussion.

defendant: Someone accused of a crime or someone who's being sued in a civil trial.

discrimination: Different, unfair treatment based on factors such as a person's race, age, religion, or gender.

evolution: The process of animals and plants slowly changing over thousands of years.

felony: A serious crime.

integrate: To make a person or group part of a larger group.

municipal: Having to do with a city or town government.

ordinance: A law or rule passed by a city or county.

prosecutor: A lawyer who prosecutes, or argues charges against an accused person in court.

segregation: The separation of people based on race, class, or ethnicity.

INDEX

WEBSITES

Due to the changing nature of Internet links, PowerKids Press has developed an online list of websites related to the subject of this book. This site is updated regularly. Please use this link to access the list: www.powerkidslinks.com/courts/state